MOJANG

MINECRAFT

DEL REY
NEW YORK

Copyright © 2018 by Mojang AB and Mojang Synergies AB. MINECRAFT is a trademark or registered trademark of Mojang Synergies AB.

All rights reserved.

Published in the United States by Del Rey, an imprint of Random House, a division of Penguin Random House LLC, New York.

DEL REY and the HOUSE colophon are registered trademarks of Penguin Random House LLC.

Published in hardcover in the United Kingdom by Egmont UK Limited.

ISBN 978-1-101-96636-5
Ebook ISBN 978-1-101-96637-2

Printed in China on acid-free paper by C & C Offset

Written by Stephanie Milton and Craig Jelley

Illustrations by Ryan Marsh, Joe Bolder & Sam Ross

randomhousebooks.com

2 4 6 8 9 7 5 3 1

First US Edition

Design by Joe Bolder

GUIDE TO:
PVP MINIGAMES

CONTENTS

1. NON-COMBAT MINIGAMES

2. COMBAT MINIGAMES

3. THE TECHNICAL STUFF

MOJANG STUFF

This super-exclusive info has come directly from the developers at Mojang.

· · · · · · · · · · · · · · · · · ·
·
·
·
This box appears next to every game in the guide. For an explanation of what each category means, and for help setting up your minigames, take a look at section 3 – The Technical Stuff – at the back of the book.

NO. OF PLAYERS	2
GAME MODE	SURVIVAL
DIFFICULTY	NORMAL
GAME TYPE	1V1
ROUND LENGTH	N/A
CLASS PLAY	ON

INTRODUCTION

Have you overcome every threat the Overworld has to throw? Do you breeze through the Nether's perils as though they were nothing? Do you scoff at the searing breath of the ender dragon? Then it's time for you to face Minecraft's most deadly challenge of all: other players! In fact, it's pretty fun to go head-to-head with other players, whatever your skill level, and this book aims to show you how! Whether you want to hone your elytra skills, test your blade against fellow combatants, prove yourself a master of mobs or a parkour pro, the builds in this guide have got something for you. Even if you're just starting out, there are tips within that'll help level the playing field between you and the experts. Now go out and win big! Just remember to be nice about it!

MARSH DAVIES
THE MOJANG TEAM

1

NON-COMBAT MINIGAMES

The minigames in this section don't involve any player-on-player fighting, but they're all about competitive fun. You can re-create these games exactly as you see them, or use them as inspiration and build on the designs with your own ideas. The only limit is your imagination!

MOB WAVES

As an experienced Minecrafter you're sure to know a thing or two about taking on a horde of hostile mobs. But in Mob Waves you'll also be competing against another player, making it doubly difficult. Positioned side by side in two lanes, it's an intense battle to see who can defeat an intimidating wave of mobs first.

HOW TO PLAY

The object of the game is to defeat all the mobs in your lane before any of them can cross the line that you're standing on, and before your opponent manages to defeat all their mobs. We'd recommend using class play for this game. To learn more about the class play system, check out pages 62–69.

NO. OF PLAYERS	2
GAME MODE	SURVIVAL
DIFFICULTY	NORMAL
GAME TYPE	1V1
ROUND LENGTH	N/A
CLASS PLAY	ON

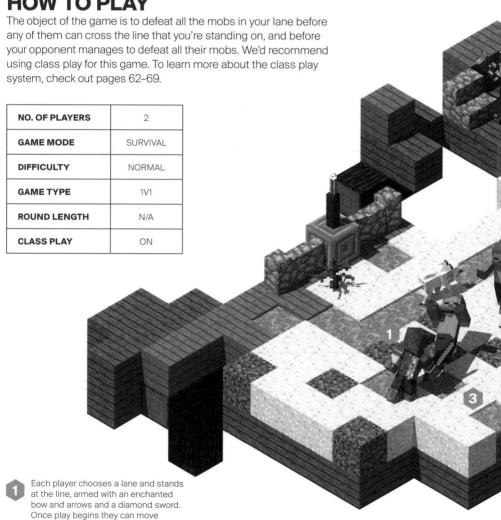

1 Each player chooses a lane and stands at the line, armed with an enchanted bow and arrows and a diamond sword. Once play begins they can move forward into their lane.

2 50 mobs are released in each lane and will make their way toward the players, who must shoot them down and prevent them from crossing the line.

TIP

Mobs like zombies and skeletons will burn in the sun. Make sure your game is built in an area where the light level is 7 or less.

3 If a player allows a mob to cross their line, they lose the game. The first player that manages to kill all their mobs wins.

OB WAVES ARENA

The concept of Mob Waves is fairly simple, but there are all sorts of fun and creative things you can do with the arena. Why not try out some of these features?

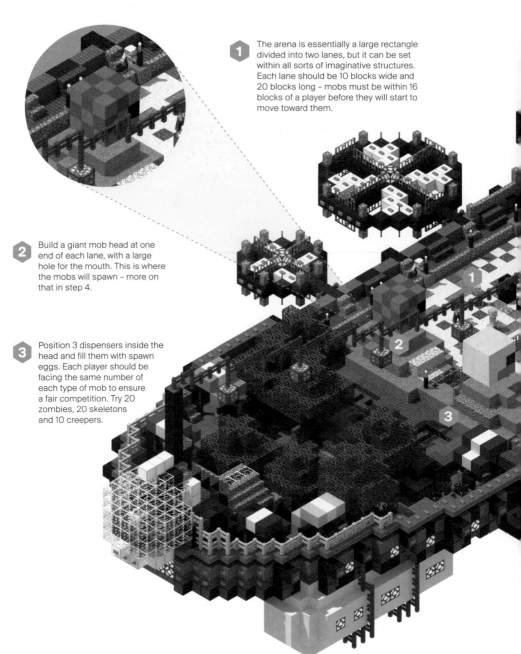

1 The arena is essentially a large rectangle divided into two lanes, but it can be set within all sorts of imaginative structures. Each lane should be 10 blocks wide and 20 blocks long – mobs must be within 16 blocks of a player before they will start to move toward them.

2 Build a giant mob head at one end of each lane, with a large hole for the mouth. This is where the mobs will spawn – more on that in step 4.

3 Position 3 dispensers inside the head and fill them with spawn eggs. Each player should be facing the same number of each type of mob to ensure a fair competition. Try 20 zombies, 20 skeletons and 10 creepers.

4 The skeleton and zombie dispensers should activate more frequently than the creeper dispenser. Create two clock circuits like the one shown below – a slow one for the creepers, and a faster one for the skeletons and zombies.

5 Run a line of iron bars between the two lanes so that they're separated but players can see what's going on in each other's lanes.

ARROW GOLF

Arrow Golf guarantees hours of fun and also offers you a chance to improve your aim with a bow. Players will be trying to shoot arrows into various holes along a challenging and unpredictable golf course, in the fewest number of shots.

HOW TO PLAY

Each player will need a bow and plenty of arrows. The aim is to get an arrow into each hole (an empty block in the ground, marked with a flag made from fence posts) on the golf course, in as few shots as possible. For each shot taken a player gains a point, and the winner is the player with the lowest score at the end of the game.

NO. OF PLAYERS	2–10
GAME MODE	CREATIVE
DIFFICULTY	NORMAL
GAME TYPE	FREE-FOR-ALL
ROUND LENGTH	N/A
CLASS PLAY	OFF

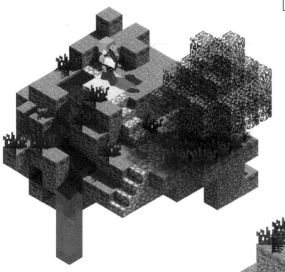

 Standing at a clearly marked starting point, the first player shoots their arrow in the direction of the first hole.

Travel to where the arrow lands and mark the spot with a block. Each player should use a different marker block to avoid confusion.

5 The game is over when everyone has finished the course. The points are added up and the person with the fewest points is the winner.

4 Players continue to take turns shooting arrows until everyone has completed the first hole. Only then can they move on to the next hole.

3 The next player takes their turn, until all players have had their first go. The first player removes the marker block from the spot where their arrow landed and stands there to take their next shot.

ARROW GOLF COURSE

Some people like a simple golf course with only a few holes, others prefer something more challenging. Whichever is the case, a decent course will always need to include a mixture of features. Let's take a look at some of the features you could incorporate into your course to make it fun and unpredictable.

1 Decide how large your course will be. A standard golf course is 18 holes, but a 4-hole course is lots of fun, too. Find a suitable spot to build it – a forest biome can work well as it's relatively flat, but green and full of trees.

2 The starting point for the course should be clearly marked. You'll want the first shot to be nice and easy, so the ground should be made from grass blocks and there should be no obstacles like long grass.

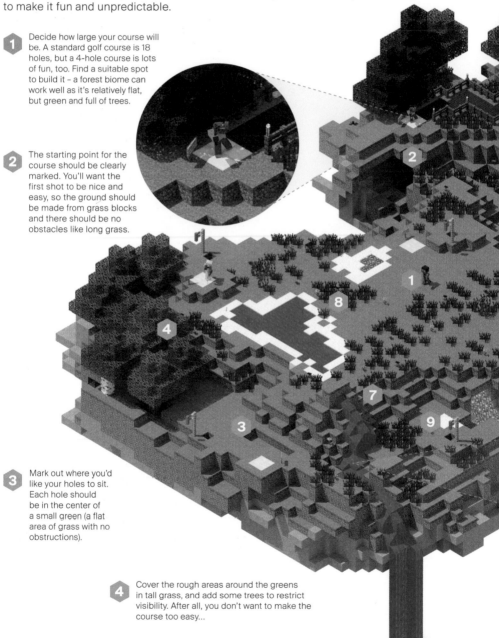

3 Mark out where you'd like your holes to sit. Each hole should be in the center of a small green (a flat area of grass with no obstructions).

4 Cover the rough areas around the greens in tall grass, and add some trees to restrict visibility. After all, you don't want to make the course too easy...

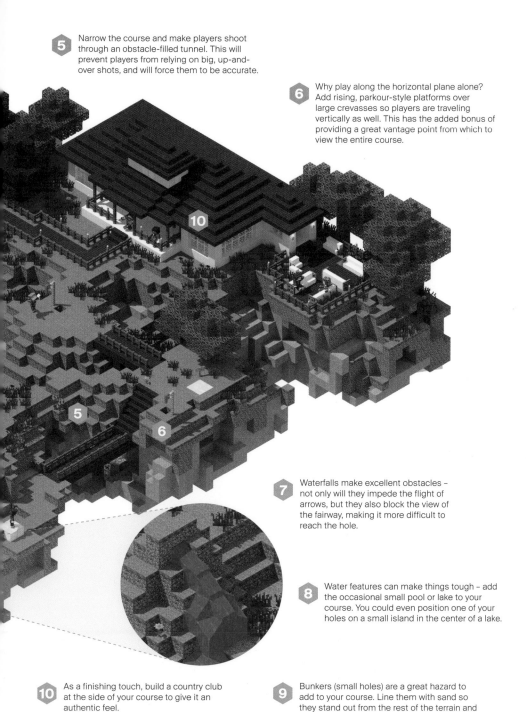

5 Narrow the course and make players shoot through an obstacle-filled tunnel. This will prevent players from relying on big, up-and-over shots, and will force them to be accurate.

6 Why play along the horizontal plane alone? Add rising, parkour-style platforms over large crevasses so players are traveling vertically as well. This has the added bonus of providing a great vantage point from which to view the entire course.

7 Waterfalls make excellent obstacles – not only will they impede the flight of arrows, but they also block the view of the fairway, making it more difficult to reach the hole.

8 Water features can make things tough – add the occasional small pool or lake to your course. You could even position one of your holes on a small island in the center of a lake.

10 As a finishing touch, build a country club at the side of your course to give it an authentic feel.

9 Bunkers (small holes) are a great hazard to add to your course. Line them with sand so they stand out from the rest of the terrain and are clearly visible to players.

HOOP SHOOT MATCH

If you're good with a bow and arrow you'll love Hoop Shoot – a frantic airborne game for two teams. Goals are scored by attackers hitting six buttons with arrows, while avoiding bow-wielding defenders and shield-bearing goalies. The first team to hit all six buttons and release the fireworks wins.

HOW TO PLAY

Players must stay on the pitch at all times during play and are not allowed to push or hit each other directly. You'll need 5 people per team and the winning team is the team that scores the most goals. All players will need elytra and firework rockets to propel them through the air. This recipe makes a non-explosive rocket that won't harm players. It's flight duration 3 – the maximum possible duration – but the recipe will also work with 2 or 1 gunpowder.

NO. OF PLAYERS	10
GAME MODE	ADVENTURE
DIFFICULTY	NORMAL
GAME TYPE	TEAM
ROUND LENGTH	N/A
CLASS PLAY	OFF

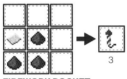

FIREWORK ROCKET RECIPE

1 Two attackers are armed with a bow and arrows, and their job is to hit each of the six buttons on the goal. When all six buttons have been hit, a dispenser is activated and explosive fireworks will be released, signaling the end of the game.

2 Two defenders work to stop the opposing team's attackers. Their job is to shoot arrows at the opposing team's attackers to prevent them from reaching the goal.

3 The goalie's job is to use their knockback-enchanted shield and sword to deflect the arrows shot by the opposing team's attackers.

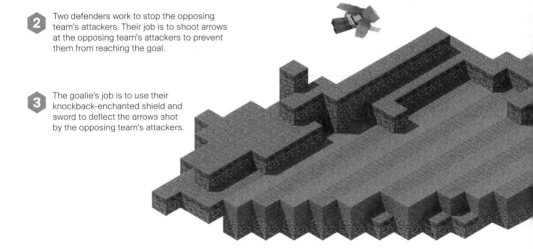

HOOP SHOOT BUILD

You'll want to create a fairly large pitch for this game, to make it exciting to play and to watch. Let's take a look at how you'll need to lay everything out.

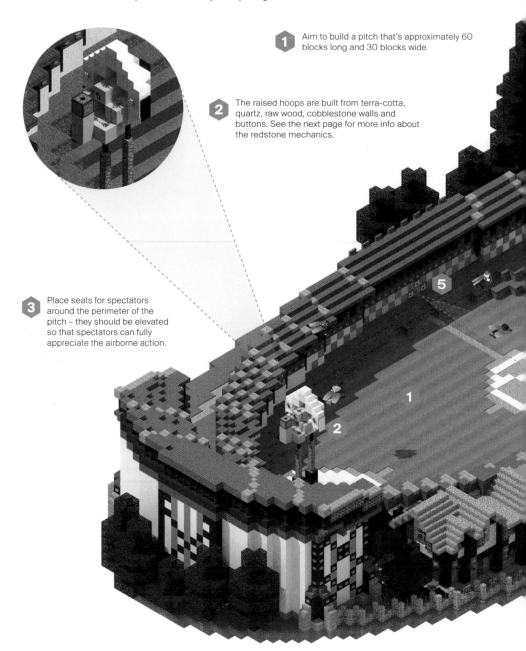

1 Aim to build a pitch that's approximately 60 blocks long and 30 blocks wide.

2 The raised hoops are built from terra-cotta, quartz, raw wood, cobblestone walls and buttons. See the next page for more info about the redstone mechanics.

3 Place seats for spectators around the perimeter of the pitch – they should be elevated so that spectators can fully appreciate the airborne action.

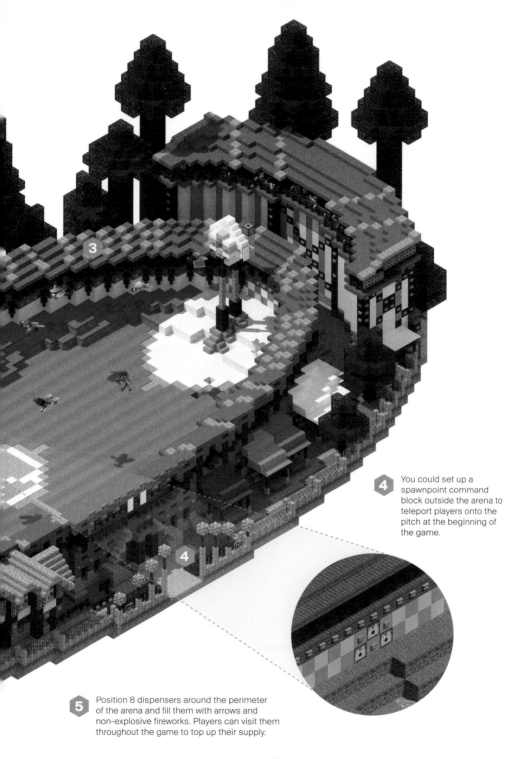

You could set up a spawnpoint command block outside the arena to teleport players onto the pitch at the beginning of the game.

Position 8 dispensers around the perimeter of the arena and fill them with arrows and non-explosive fireworks. Players can visit them throughout the game to top up their supply.

HOOP SHOOT REDSTONE MECHANICS

In order to set off the explosive fireworks you'll need to build a simple redstone mechanism behind each hoop. This will activate the dispenser when all the buttons have been shot, releasing the fireworks. Follow this step-by-step guide to put the finishing touches to this exciting game.

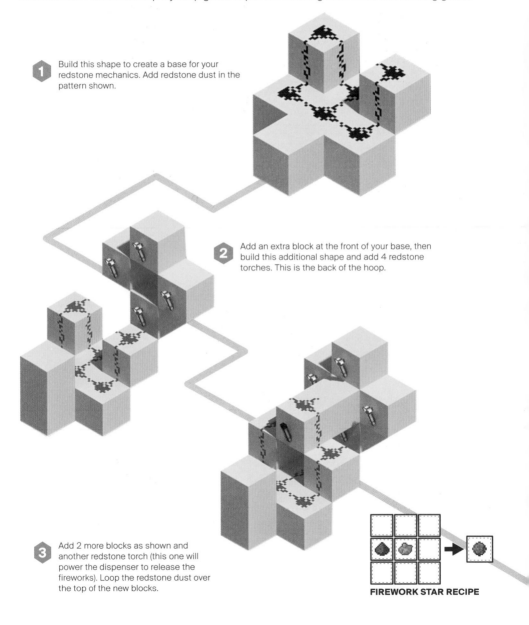

1 Build this shape to create a base for your redstone mechanics. Add redstone dust in the pattern shown.

2 Add an extra block at the front of your base, then build this additional shape and add 4 redstone torches. This is the back of the hoop.

3 Add 2 more blocks as shown and another redstone torch (this one will power the dispenser to release the fireworks). Loop the redstone dust over the top of the new blocks.

FIREWORK STAR RECIPE

6 This is what the front of the hoop should look like when you've finished. Don't forget to add all 6 buttons.

5 Now you can build the rest of your hoop. This is what it will look like from the back. Don't forget to add 2 more redstone torches.

4 Place your dispenser, making sure it's facing up toward the sky, and fill it with explosive fireworks. You'll need to craft firework stars, then combine those with paper and gunpowder.

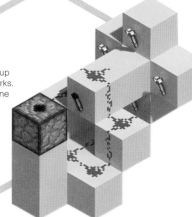

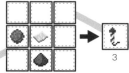

3

FIREWORK ROCKET RECIPE

ELYTRA ACE

In this minigame you'll be competing with other players to navigate a series of dangerous obstacles and make it to the end of the course. You'll be doing this while gliding on elytra and being propelled by fireworks. Oh, and your opponents will be attempting to push you off course as you go. There's a lot going on!

HOW TO PLAY

The object of the game is to make it through the course unscathed and reach the end zone before your opponents.

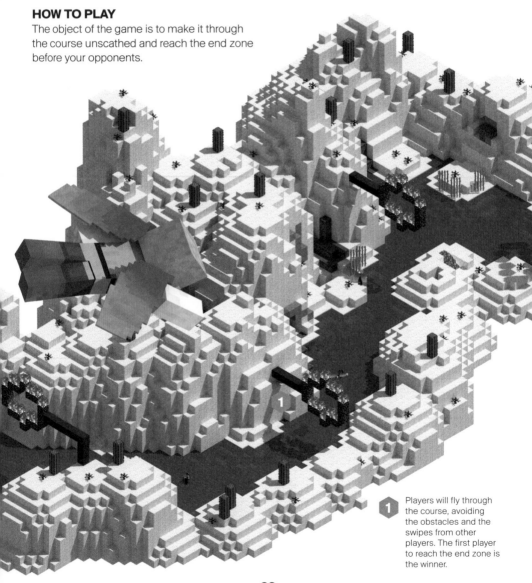

1 Players will fly through the course, avoiding the obstacles and the swipes from other players. The first player to reach the end zone is the winner.

NO. OF PLAYERS	2-10
GAME MODE	ADVENTURE
DIFFICULTY	NORMAL
GAME TYPE	FREE-FOR-ALL
ROUND LENGTH	N/A
CLASS PLAY	OFF

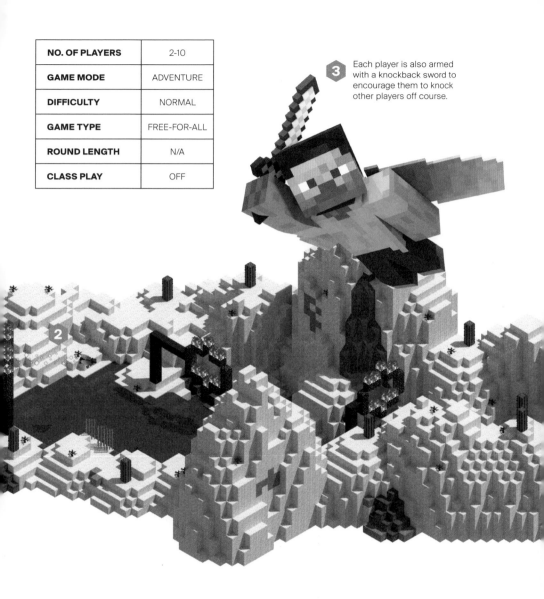

3 Each player is also armed with a knockback sword to encourage them to knock other players off course.

2 Each player is given a pair of elytra and a stack of non-explosive firework rockets (see page 16) to propel them through the course.

MOJANG STUFF

One of our all-time favorite community maps is Terra Swoop Force, made by Noxcrew for Java Edition. It's a brilliant, breathless elytra-powered descent into the center of the earth, with plenty of stalagmites and stalactites to faceplant into! Seek it out!

ELYTRA ACE BUILD

Your Elytra Ace course should be challenging, but not impossible. The key to a good course is to include a mixture of features and surprising obstacles to keep players on their toes.

 Use consistent checkpoints, like rings of a certain color, to mark out the route along the course. This will prevent players from flying around aimlessly and makes for a more competitive race.

2 The course can dip into the terrain – you could use natural ravines as winding routes within the larger course, and add canopies over the top.

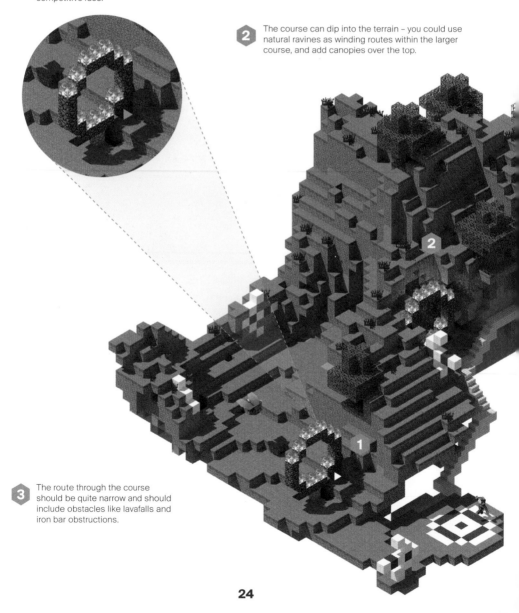

3 The route through the course should be quite narrow and should include obstacles like lavafalls and iron bar obstructions.

4 Eye-catching features will distract players and make the course more challenging. Use bright colors to create fun builds throughout the course. Giant mobs are always popular – the course could even run through the mouth of a giant dragon.

5 Include plenty of sharp turns and even a few vertical drops to keep players on their toes.

WOOL RACE

Grab your shears and dive into pens full of obliging sheep to relieve them of their woolly coats. The aim is to gather more colored wool blocks than your opponents. Not all colors of wool are equal, though, and you'll need to move quickly and make some strategic decisions about which sheep to target.

HOW TO PLAY

The object of Wool Race is to shear as much wool as possible in the time allowed. Players have five minutes to shear as much wool as they can and place it in their designated chest within the pen. Chests are labeled with numbers 1, 2, 3 and 4, and each player will need to choose a number before the game begins. Players must place the wool in the chest for it to count. Players are not allowed to hit or push one another during the game.

NO. OF PLAYERS	2-4
GAME MODE	SURVIVAL
DIFFICULTY	PEACEFUL
GAME TYPE	FREE-FOR-ALL
ROUND LENGTH	5 MINUTES
CLASS PLAY	OFF

Each color of wool is worth a different number of points and the winner is the player who has the highest number of points at the end of the game. Make sure all players know how many points each color is worth – you could use the values below or create your own system.

WHITE – 1 point

RED – 2 points

YELLOW – 3 points

BLUE – 4 points

GREEN – 5 points

PURPLE – 6 points

WOOL RACE BUILD

Splitting your pens over several levels will ensure maximum fun. You'll want enough space for at least 100 sheep, and throwing in various obstacles will make the map more challenging to navigate. This setup will give you some inspiration.

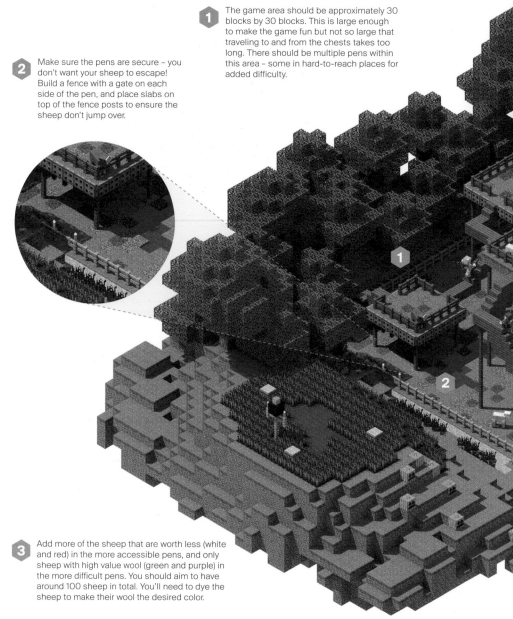

1 The game area should be approximately 30 blocks by 30 blocks. This is large enough to make the game fun but not so large that traveling to and from the chests takes too long. There should be multiple pens within this area – some in hard-to-reach places for added difficulty.

2 Make sure the pens are secure – you don't want your sheep to escape! Build a fence with a gate on each side of the pen, and place slabs on top of the fence posts to ensure the sheep don't jump over.

3 Add more of the sheep that are worth less (white and red) in the more accessible pens, and only sheep with high value wool (green and purple) in the more difficult pens. You should aim to have around 100 sheep in total. You'll need to dye the sheep to make their wool the desired color.

4 Various obstacles can be added to the pen to make navigating a little more difficult for players – try planting clusters of trees and adding small lakes.

6 Finish off the build by constructing a barn to make players feel like they're on a real farm.

5 Chests should be clearly labeled with large numbers 1-4 to avoid any confusion – you don't want players placing wool in someone else's chest. Chests should be as far away from one another as possible – you could place one at each corner of the pen.

2

COMBAT MINIGAMES

The games in this section are ideal for players who thrive on the thrill of PVP (player-versus-player) combat. Whether it's battling one-on-one with your friends, fighting against an enemy team or engaging in a frantic free-for-all, there's a combat minigame to suit everyone.

SKYWARS

Take to the skies and battle for your life on a cluster of perilous floating islands. Players will be competing against one another to gather resources while fending off enemy attacks and trying not to get knocked off solid ground to their doom. The winner is the last man standing.

HOW TO PLAY

At the start of the game players have an empty inventory and no armor – they'll need to collect whatever equipment they can find on the islands to survive. Once equipped, players turn on one another and take one another out using whatever means necessary.

NO. OF PLAYERS	2-10
GAME MODE	SURVIVAL
DIFFICULTY	PEACEFUL
GAME TYPE	FREE-FOR-ALL
ROUND LENGTH	N/A
CLASS PLAY	OFF

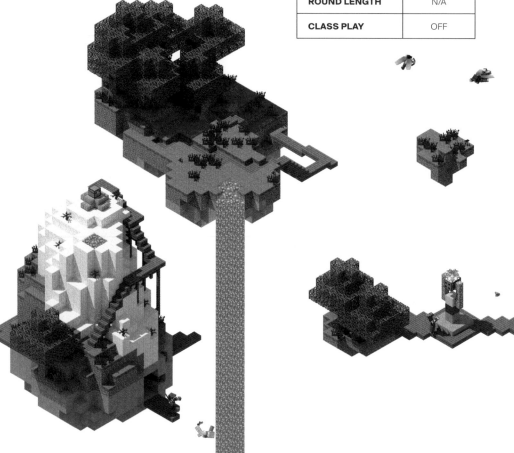

SKYWARS ISLANDS

Skywars is a great opportunity to get creative. You can cover the islands with interesting features and useful resources, and you can have fun making it as difficult as possible for players to move between them. Let's take a look at some of the features you might want to include.

Many people choose to build one large, central island with smaller islands encircling it. Some of the outer islands could be connected by narrow walkways, but the central island is usually isolated to make it more difficult to reach.

If you decide to link some islands via walkways, make them one block wide so it's easy for players to be knocked off. And they don't have to be complete – there could be gaps in some places to make it particularly dangerous.

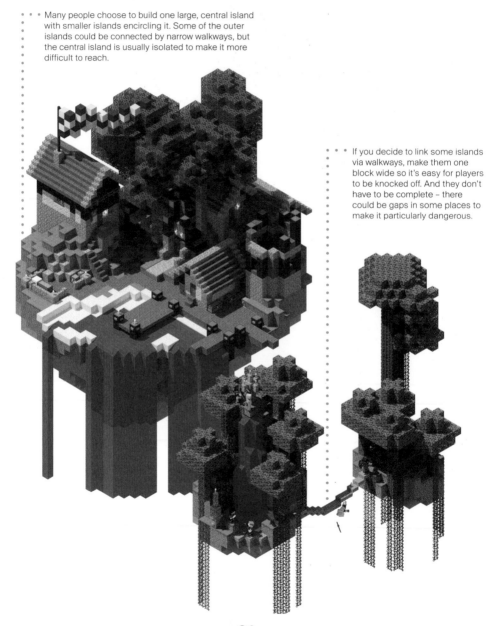

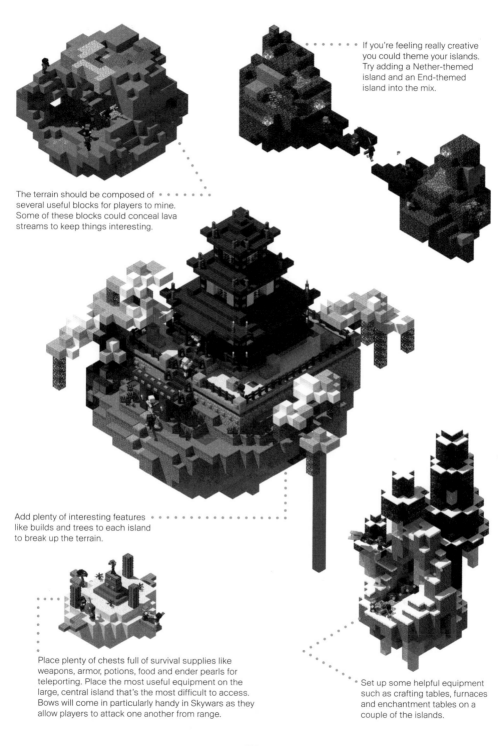

If you're feeling really creative you could theme your islands. Try adding a Nether-themed island and an End-themed island into the mix.

The terrain should be composed of several useful blocks for players to mine. Some of these blocks could conceal lava streams to keep things interesting.

Add plenty of interesting features like builds and trees to each island to break up the terrain.

Place plenty of chests full of survival supplies like weapons, armor, potions, food and ender pearls for teleporting. Place the most useful equipment on the large, central island that's the most difficult to access. Bows will come in particularly handy in Skywars as they allow players to attack one another from range.

Set up some helpful equipment such as crafting tables, furnaces and enchantment tables on a couple of the islands.

SPLEEF TOURNAMENT

The aim of Spleef is to quite literally take the floor out from under your opponents' feet. Players jump around an elevated arena floor, attempting to destroy the blocks directly under the other players' feet and send them plummeting to their demise. It's brutal and it's fun!

HOW TO PLAY

Each player will need an inventory full of shovels, but no other equipment is permitted. The goal is to send the other players falling through the arena floor and into a pit by mining the blocks under their feet. Players will need to move quickly, think strategically and remember to keep an eye on their own footing. The last player standing is the winner.

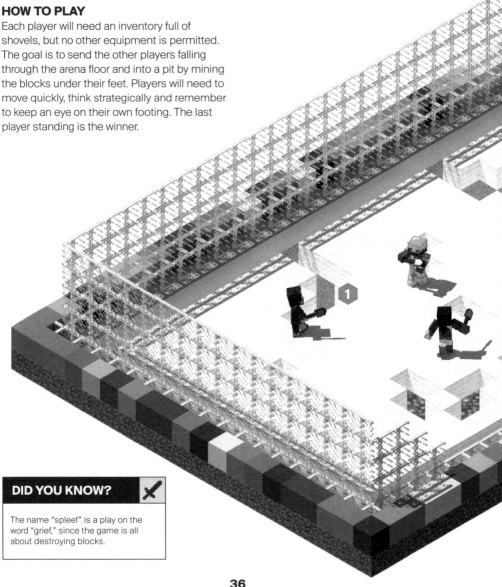

DID YOU KNOW?

The name "spleef" is a play on the word "grief," since the game is all about destroying blocks.

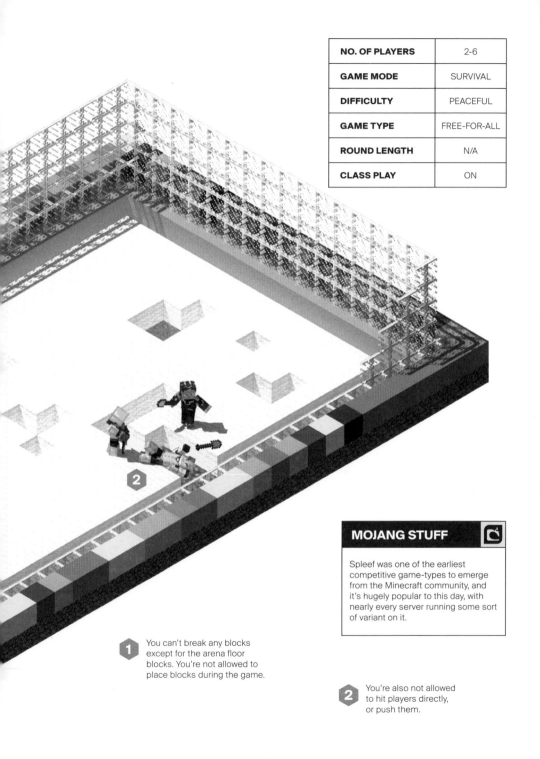

NO. OF PLAYERS	2-6
GAME MODE	SURVIVAL
DIFFICULTY	PEACEFUL
GAME TYPE	FREE-FOR-ALL
ROUND LENGTH	N/A
CLASS PLAY	ON

MOJANG STUFF

Spleef was one of the earliest competitive game-types to emerge from the Minecraft community, and it's hugely popular to this day, with nearly every server running some sort of variant on it.

1 You can't break any blocks except for the arena floor blocks. You're not allowed to place blocks during the game.

2 You're also not allowed to hit players directly, or push them.

SPLEEF ARENA BUILD

You'll need to build the floor of the Spleef arena out of blocks that are easy to break with a shovel – most people choose snow or clay, but you can also use dirt or wool. Let's take a look at how best to construct a Spleef arena.

1 You could set up a spawnpoint command block just outside the arena (see page 77 for a tutorial). Players can then hit the button when they're ready to teleport onto the arena floor at the beginning of the game.

2 It's a good idea to build high walls around your arena so that players aren't tempted to escape before the end of the game. You can build simple walls or have fun with different colors and blocks.

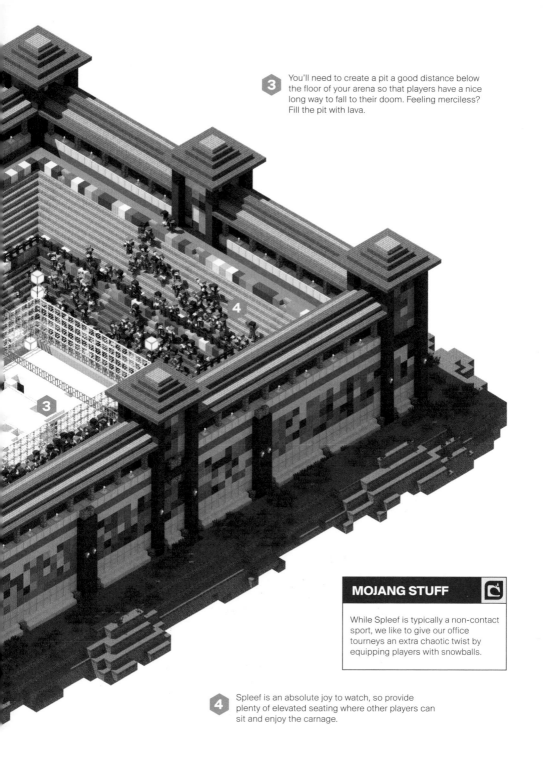

You'll need to create a pit a good distance below the floor of your arena so that players have a nice long way to fall to their doom. Feeling merciless? Fill the pit with lava.

MOJANG STUFF

While Spleef is typically a non-contact sport, we like to give our office tourneys an extra chaotic twist by equipping players with snowballs.

Spleef is an absolute joy to watch, so provide plenty of elevated seating where other players can sit and enjoy the carnage.

CAPTURE THE FLAG

The concept of this popular minigame is simple: capture the enemy team's flag and rebuild it inside your own base before they can do the same with yours. You'll need to think strategically if you hope to circumvent the enemy team's defenses and infiltrate their base whilst simultaneously protecting your own flag.

HOW TO PLAY

Once players have been divided into teams and released into the arena, the only blocks they are permitted to break are the blocks that make up the enemy team's flag. The winner is the first team to destroy their enemy's flag, take it back to their base and rebuild it in their own flag room.

NO. OF PLAYERS	6-10
GAME MODE	SURVIVAL
DIFFICULTY	PEACEFUL
GAME TYPE	TEAM
ROUND LENGTH	N/A
CLASS PLAY	ON

TIP

To distinguish between the teams, you could provide dyed leather helmets that correspond to the team's color, e.g., red for a red team and blue for a blue team.

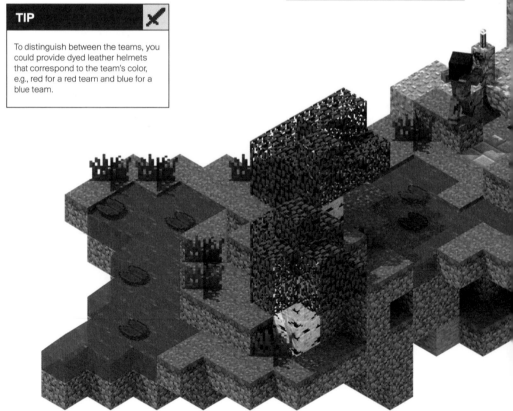

40

CAPTURE THE FLAG MAP BUILD

Create two identical bases and place them in a reasonably symmetrical map to make gameplay as fair as possible. You might want to use the clone command – see pages 72-73 for a tutorial. Let's take a look at some of the features you could include within the map.

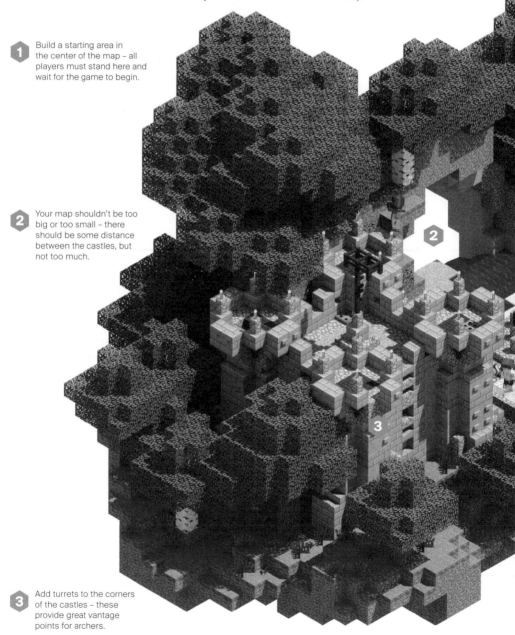

1 Build a starting area in the center of the map – all players must stand here and wait for the game to begin.

2 Your map shouldn't be too big or too small – there should be some distance between the castles, but not too much.

3 Add turrets to the corners of the castles – these provide great vantage points for archers.

4 Think about adding interesting landscape features (small settlements, lava pools, etc.).

5 Build your flags from red and blue wool. Position each flag at the top of a turret in the center of each base to make it as difficult to reach as possible.

6 Try to make it as difficult as possible to infiltrate each castle – build an outer wall around the base with one narrow entry point.

7 Position some trees around the castles to help obscure players' views and make attacking and defending more interesting.

CAPTURE THE FLAG CASTLE DEFENSES

Once the game begins, resourceful players will probably want to add their own defenses to their castles. To encourage everyone to get creative you could add chests full of supplies somewhere inside each castle. Take a look at the features on this page and stock the chests accordingly.

1 Create a lava drop with a lever, activated sticky pistons and stone blocks. Create a ring of stone blocks with pistons surrounding it underneath. Join the pistons to a lever with redstone dust and place a stone block on the end of each. Pour lava into the small bowl that this has created. When you pull the lever, the stone blocks will be retracted by the pistons and pour hot lava on invaders passing below.

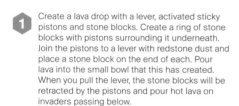

2 To give your team a distance advantage, dig out a 5-block-long ditch in the castle hallway, covering the width of the hall. Make it 4 blocks deep, and add cactus or lava at the bottom. Add small walls to the side that you'll be defending from to provide cover while you shoot arrows at the attackers.

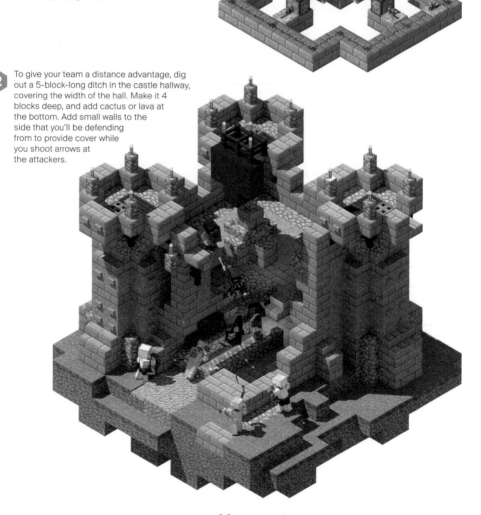

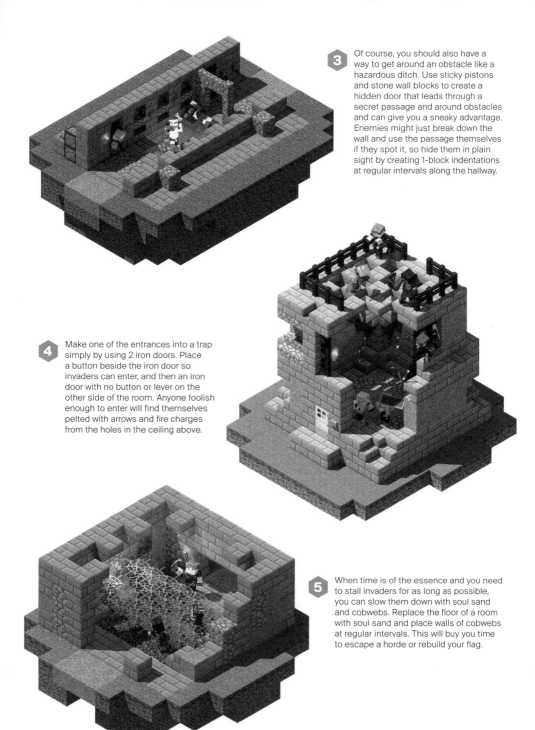

3 Of course, you should also have a way to get around an obstacle like a hazardous ditch. Use sticky pistons and stone wall blocks to create a hidden door that leads through a secret passage and around obstacles and can give you a sneaky advantage. Enemies might just break down the wall and use the passage themselves if they spot it, so hide them in plain sight by creating 1-block indentations at regular intervals along the hallway.

4 Make one of the entrances into a trap simply by using 2 iron doors. Place a button beside the iron door so invaders can enter, and then an iron door with no button or lever on the other side of the room. Anyone foolish enough to enter will find themselves pelted with arrows and fire charges from the holes in the ceiling above.

5 When time is of the essence and you need to stall invaders for as long as possible, you can slow them down with soul sand and cobwebs. Replace the floor of a room with soul sand and place walls of cobwebs at regular intervals. This will buy you time to escape a horde or rebuild your flag.

GLADIATOR COMBAT

Inspired by the ancient Roman sport, Gladiator Combat is a fight to the death to determine which player is the greatest warrior. Gladiators must compete for possession of weapons, then use what they have to finish off the other players.

HOW TO PLAY

There are very few rules for Gladiator Combat. The object of the game is to defeat the other players and be the last gladiator standing. Anything goes, really.

NO. OF PLAYERS	2-10
GAME MODE	SURVIVAL
DIFFICULTY	NORMAL
GAME TYPE	FREE-FOR-ALL
ROUND LENGTH	N/A
CLASS PLAY	OFF

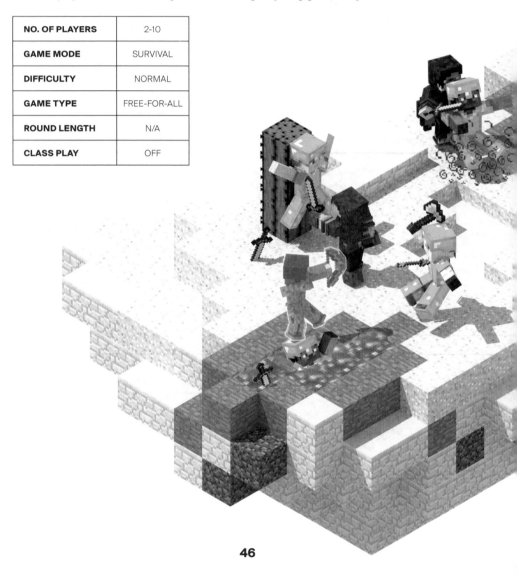

Players step into the arena armed with nothing. They'll need to make a dash for chests containing various weapons and armor that are positioned around the arena and grab what they can before their opponents swipe everything. Once in the arena, players are not permitted to leave until the battle is over and the winner announced.

TIP

Since anything goes in Gladiator Combat, you might want to have players team up and keep score of their kills for an added level of competition. To learn how to set up a scoring system using the scoreboard command, see pages 74-76.

AMPHITHEATER BUILD

Gladiator combat traditionally took place in enormous amphitheaters with raised seating where spectators could watch the show. This build is on a smaller scale, but it includes plenty of features that will make for a dramatic spectacle. It will suit your minigame perfectly!

1 The seating area should be raised above the arena floor so that everyone has a clear view of the action.

2 Chests containing a variety of weapons, armor, helpful potions and harmful splash potions should be distributed across the arena.

3 Strategically placed cacti present another hazard – gladiators can push one another into them to inflict yet more damage.

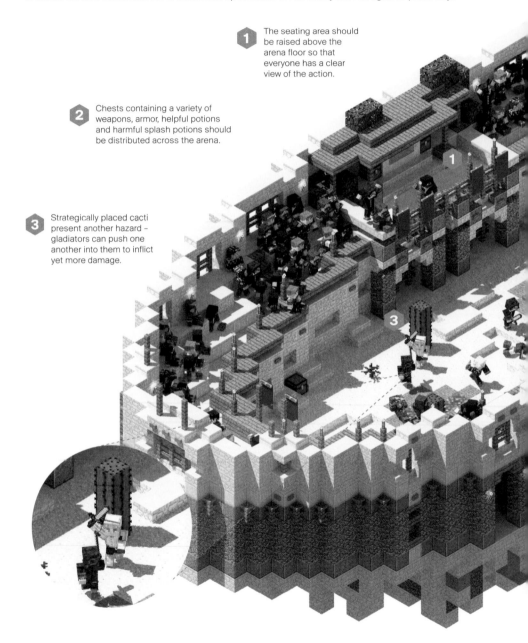

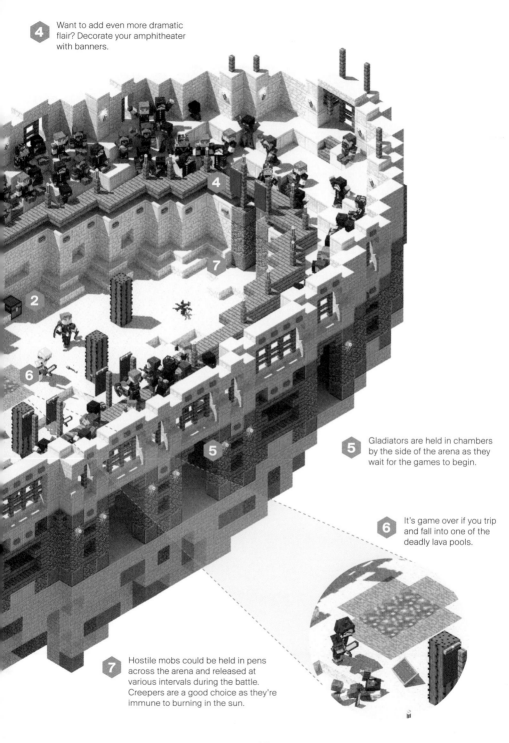

4 Want to add even more dramatic flair? Decorate your amphitheater with banners.

5 Gladiators are held in chambers by the side of the arena as they wait for the games to begin.

6 It's game over if you trip and fall into one of the deadly lava pools.

7 Hostile mobs could be held in pens across the arena and released at various intervals during the battle. Creepers are a good choice as they're immune to burning in the sun.

BATTLE PARKOUR

Parkour requires skill, precision and nerves of steel – players must jump across a challenging arena of floating platforms without falling. Battle Parkour has all the fun of regular parkour with the additional excitement of PVP combat.

HOW TO PLAY

The first player to reach the arena's end zone is the winner. PVP combat is encouraged – players can try to knock their opponents off the platforms. Placing blocks is, of course, forbidden.

NO. OF PLAYERS	2-10
GAME MODE	SURVIVAL
DIFFICULTY	PEACEFUL
GAME TYPE	FREE-FOR-ALL
ROUND LENGTH	N/A
CLASS PLAY	OFF

BATTLE PARKOUR ARENA

Parkour arenas must be carefully planned – each jump will need to be tested as it's built to make sure it's achievable. You can have lots of fun with the design, though – let's take a look at some features that will make your parkour arena a great experience.

1 Jumps should be difficult but not impossible – vary the space between platforms and use single-block platforms for maximum difficulty.

2 It's a good idea to add checkpoints – that way, if players miss a jump they will respawn at the last checkpoint they hit rather than back at the beginning. See page 77 for a tutorial.

3 Vary the blocks you use to build your platforms to make the course more fun. You can use everything from bouncy slime blocks and mob heads to invisible barrier blocks and cactus blocks that will inflict damage.

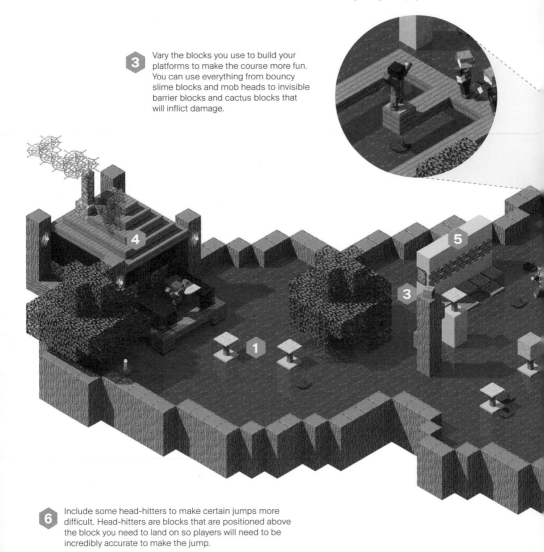

6 Include some head-hitters to make certain jumps more difficult. Head-hitters are blocks that are positioned above the block you need to land on so players will need to be incredibly accurate to make the jump.

5 Work in some redstone elements where possible to take competitors by surprise. This narrow ledge has frequent pressure plates, which activate pistons that can push the less agile players off the course. Just make sure there's an easy way to get back on track nearby.

7 Throw some ladder jumps into the mix – these are platforms where the player will have to aim to land on a ladder placed on the side of a block.

3

THE TECHNICAL STUFF

Need a little help setting up your minigame? Whether you're new to multiplayer or you're a more seasoned player looking for a quick refresher, this section can help. Read on for a walkthrough of everything from setting up a basic multiplayer game to using command blocks.

CONNECTING WITH OTHER PLAYERS

Minecraft was designed to be a multiplayer game so players could share the fun, and it's easy to connect with others. There are several ways to play multiplayer – here's a quick reminder of the options so you can decide which one is right for you.

LOCAL AREA NETWORK GAMES

Minecraft's local area network (LAN) feature allows people on the same network/router to connect with one another and play minigames together. This is the option to use if you want to play with other people in the same building – you can use the LAN feature on computer and pocket editions.

Load the world you'd like to open to LAN, then go back to the main menu. Click settings, multiplayer, and choose multiplayer and visible to LAN players to make your world visible to other players on your network. Up to four players can play together on a LAN.

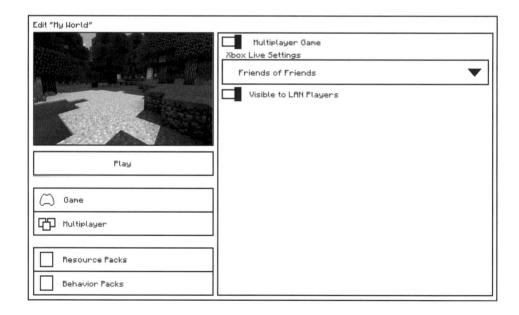

SERVERS

Servers are huge online worlds, created by Minecraft's official, trusted partners – nice community members, just like you. There are all kinds of servers and each offers a different fun experience – you'll find everything from custom worlds ready to be explored to imaginative minigames where you can compete with your friends.

You can join a server on Windows 10, mobile devices and tablets, Xbox One and Nintendo Switch. You can connect to a server from anywhere in the world – all you need is an internet connection and a free Xbox Live account (you don't need to own an Xbox to set up an account). If you're an Xbox One player you'll need an Xbox Live Gold subscription to play multiplayer.

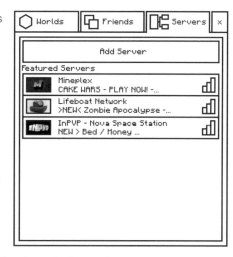

Click play, then click on the servers tab. You'll see a list of popular featured servers – just choose the one you'd like to join and start playing.

ONLINE GAMES

If you want to share a game with players who aren't in the same building, open the menu and click on invite to game. You'll be taken to the Xbox Live screen where you can see all your friends who have an Xbox account. From here you can choose which friends to invite to your game – they can be anywhere in the world and they'll be able to connect to your game.

To join a friend's online game, go to the friends tab. You'll be able to see all joinable Realms and friends here, then you can choose which one you want to join.

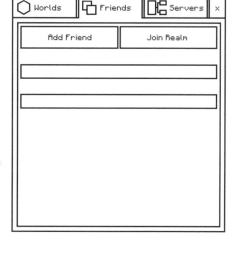

REALMS

Many minigame creators choose to share their maps via Realms. Realms are official Mojang-run servers that provide an easy and safe way for players to have fun together. They're always online and they belong to you.

HOW REALMS WORK

Depending on how creative you're feeling you can either play on a friend's Realm, on a pre-existing Realm template, or you can get creative and make your own. It's up to you! Realms are super secure – they're just for you and your friends, and only people invited by the owner of the Realm can join. A Realm is always accessible, even when the owner logs off. Up to ten people can play on a Realm at once, and only the owner needs to pay – their friends can play on it for free.

CONNECTING TO REALMS

You'll need to be on a computer, mobile device or Xbox to connect to Realms. Open Minecraft and click play, then create new, then new Realm, then create new Realm.

CUSTOMIZING YOUR REALM

So you've decided to set up your own Realm to share with your friends. That's great! Once you're connected to Realms you get to make all sorts of decisions that will help customize your world, make it unique and dictate how your minigame will work.

GAME SETTINGS

To access the following settings, enter the settings menu either from the pencil icon next to your Realm or by going to the menu screen when in your world and then going to settings.

Go to game mode and choose Creative for non-combat games where you don't need to limit players' inventories. Choose Adventure to prevent players from breaking blocks.

You can change the name of your Realm in the game menu.

Go to game mode and choose Survival for minigames involving hostile mobs or PVP battles.

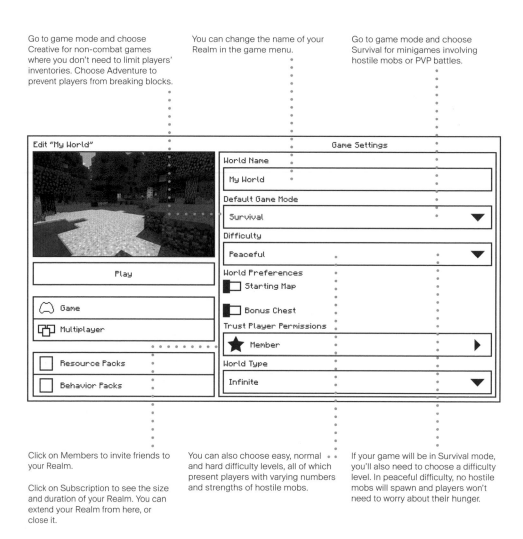

Click on Members to invite friends to your Realm.

Click on Subscription to see the size and duration of your Realm. You can extend your Realm from here, or close it.

You can also choose easy, normal and hard difficulty levels, all of which present players with varying numbers and strengths of hostile mobs.

If your game will be in Survival mode, you'll also need to choose a difficulty level. In peaceful difficulty, no hostile mobs will spawn and players won't need to worry about their hunger.

GAME TYPE

Although you won't find game type listed in the settings menu, it's something you'll need to think about. Your choice will depend on the number of players you want to include and how you'd like them to interact with one another. Here are the options.

1 V 1

1 V 1 games are intended for two players who want to play competitively against each other.

TEAM

Team games allow teams of up to five players to play against one another.

FREE-FOR-ALL

Free-for-all games are for three or more players, and it's every player for themselves.

DID YOU KNOW?

Realms is a subscription service, so make sure you get a parent or guardian's permission before you sign up. To find out more and get a free trial, visit https://minecraft.ent/en-us/realms/.

THE CHARACTER CLASS SYSTEM

Ever played minigames with friends who are much more experienced than you and who quickly obliterate you with their pro moves? Incorporating a character class system will level the playing field so that everyone can enjoy minigames together, no matter how experienced they are. Here's an example to inspire you.

In this system there are six characters to choose from. The warrior and the mage are best suited to beginners, the ninja and support archer are ideal for players with a little more experience and the pyro tank and the engineer are perfect for advanced players.

Each character has different strengths and weaknesses and a unique inventory that will dictate a certain approach to playing PVP minigames. The characters are all balanced against one another so that no one player has a distinct advantage over the others.

Character classes can be used in many battle minigames, but there are some games for which they may not work so well. For example, in Gladiator Combat, players collect as many resources as they can before battles begin, so this may allow some classes to gain an item that once gave another class an edge.

TIP

The character class system can be used exactly as detailed in this section, or you can use it as inspiration to create your own unique system. It's your minigame, after all!

TIP

You'll find a note on each of the minigame pages earlier in this book, telling you whether class play is appropriate for that particular game.

You'll need to decide whether you're happy for players to pick any class (potentially resulting in several players of the same class), or if each player must choose a different class. You'll also need to decide who gets to choose first and whether you trust players not to cheat or if you'll need to police them as they collect their equipment!

BEGINNER CLASS: THE WARRIOR

The all-rounder of this character class system, the warrior has solid armor, a powerful sword and a good supply of healing items. They also have the ability to spawn and tame wolves to fight alongside them and help them defeat their opponents.

STATS

⚔ **STRENGTH**	4
👕 **DEFENSE**	5
🦵 **SPEED**	2
❤ **HEALING**	1
🧤 **MAGIC**	1

EQUIPMENT

Diamond Sword	Potion of Fire Resistance	Potion of Regeneration	Potion of Swiftness	Potion of Healing	Potion of Healing	Bucket of Milk	Wolf Egg	Bone
							3	10

ARMOR

Golden Helmet	Golden Chestplate	Golden Pants	Golden Boots

TACTICS

The warrior is an offensive powerhouse. The diamond sword makes light work of opponents, and warriors should be able to defeat most enemies in a one-on-one battle thanks to the protection of their gold armor. When damaged, warriors should seek cover and take time to heal before returning to the fray.

SPECIAL MOVE – RABID ALLIES

Throw down the three wolf spawn eggs and tame each one with bones before charging into battle. The wolves will help distract your enemies as you use your sword to finish them off.

BEGINNER CLASS: THE MAGE

The mage is a powerful conjurer able to summon forces of both good and evil to cause havoc on the battlefield. Equipped with a number of splash potions and potentially dangerous blocks, they can easily inflict damage on enemies that are unfortunate enough to cross their path.

STATS

⚔ STRENGTH	1
🛡 DEFENSE	2
👢 SPEED	3
❤ HEALING	4
🧪 MAGIC	5

EQUIPMENT

Totem of Undying	Harming (Splash)	Weakness (Splash)	Poison (Splash)	Slowness (Splash)	Iron Block 4	Soul Sand 32	Magma 10	Enderman Spawn Egg 3

ARMOR

Jack o' Lantern	Leather Chestplate	Leather Leggings	Leather Boots

TACTICS

The mage has very little defense, so attacking from a safe distance is their go-to move. But death is not the end for the mage thanks to their totem of undying. Mages can also summon endermen to attack any player on the map, or sacrifice their jack o'lantern helmet and construct an iron golem instead.

SPECIAL MOVE – SLOW DEATH

Find a small, obscured area, e.g., behind a door, and replace the floor blocks with soul sand before locating a good hiding spot nearby. When an enemy enters the area, the soul sand will slow them down, giving the mage the opportunity to pelt them with splash potions before they can escape.

INTERMEDIATE CLASS: THE NINJA

An agile class with a number of potions at its disposal, the ninja excels in speeding from one skirmish to the next. Ninjas do not wear armor, so they should attack quickly and inflict as much damage as possible before retreating to a safe distance to regroup.

STATS

⚔ STRENGTH		3
🛡 DEFENSE		1
👟 SPEED		5
❤ HEALING		1
✋ MAGIC		3

EQUIPMENT

Golden Sword	Ender Pearl	Harming (Lingering)	Poison (Lingering)	Weakness (Lingering)	Slowness (Lingering)	Healing (Lingering)	Strength (Lingering)	Swiftness (Lingering)
	10							

ARMOR

	Elytra	

TACTICS

The ninja's golden sword may not be the most powerful weapon, but combined with some harmful lingering potions it can deal a fatal blow. The ninja excels in maneuverability, whether soaring on elytra or darting across arenas using ender pearls, making it a very difficult class for enemies to lock on to and to damage.

SPECIAL MOVE – RAIN OF FIRE

With the help of their elytra the ninja soars over the battlefield, dropping lingering potions indiscriminately on the ground below. The result is chaos for the ninja's foes, and often for their allies, too, so sensible ninjas would do well to warn their teammates before they deploy this tactic.

INTERMEDIATE CLASS: THE SUPPORT ARCHER

The support archer is a hybrid of a classic archer and a medic. They have little in the way of defense, so they rely on their bow to cause or cure damage from a safe distance. In an emergency the archer can fall back on their rudimentary sword to get themselves out of a tight spot.

STATS

⚔ STRENGTH		2
🛡 DEFENSE		2
👖 SPEED		3
❤ HEALING		5
✋ MAGIC		3

EQUIPMENT

| Bow | Wooden Sword | Arrow (64) | Spectral Arrow (10) | Potion of Invisibility | Tipped Arrow of Slowness (10) | Tipped Arrow of Poison (10) | Tipped Arrow of Healing (10) | Tipped Arrow of Strength (10) |

ARMOR

| Leather Helmet | Leather Chestplate | Leather Pants | Leather Boots |

TACTICS

The support archer attacks at range, supplementing the melee attacks of his teammates. In this way the archer is able to provide beneficial status effects to teammates with tipped arrows, or mark weaker opponents with spectral arrows to help teammates finish them off.

SPECIAL MOVE – HIDDEN HELPER

The support archer drinks a potion of invisibility and moves across the battlefield undetected. The archer is able to locate allies in need and bestow helpful status effects using tipped arrows. If there are no allies to help, the archer can always launch more lethal arrows at enemy players and deal invisible damage.

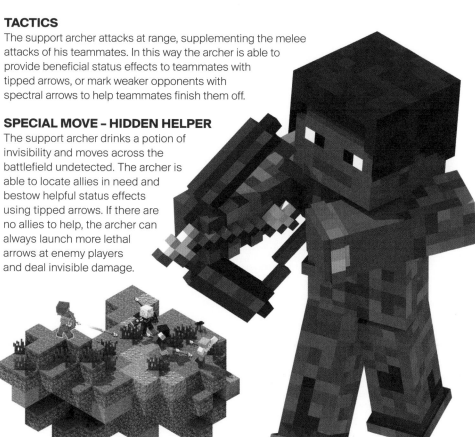

ADVANCED CLASS: THE ENGINEER

With less-than-impressive weaponry and only average armor, the engineer seems like a sitting duck at first, but the strength of this character class lies in its ingenuity. The engineer has the tools to create contraptions that are more effective than any weapon that can be stored in an inventory.

STATS

⚔ STRENGTH		3
👕 DEFENSE		3
👖 SPEED		1
❤ HEALING		1
✋ MAGIC		3

EQUIPMENT

Wooden Sword	Redstone Dust (32)	Pressure Plate (5)	Piston (10)	Slime Block (10)	Dispenser (5)	Arrow (64)	Fire Charge (10)	TNT (5)

ARMOR

Iron Helmet	Iron Chestplate	Iron Leggings	Iron Boots

TACTICS

The engineer operates in secret, working on deadly mechanisms that will later be used to defeat enemies. Fire charges and TNT can be used in close combat, but retaliation is likely and the engineer isn't built to withstand much damage.

SPECIAL MOVE – CHAIN REACTION

The engineer tunnels under the battleground, planting blocks of TNT and linking them together using redstone. A pressure plate is placed above the central-most block of TNT. When an unwitting victim steps on the pressure plate the entire line of TNT will detonate. It would be wise to warn teammates that this attack is imminent to give them the opportunity to flee the area – this move is best saved for truly dire circumstances.

ADVANCED CLASS: THE PYRO TANK

With axe and shield in hand, and dressed in sturdy diamond armor, the pyro tank is a powerhouse that many will struggle to overcome. Though it lacks any truly deadly weapons, the pyro tank has a clever combination of resources that together produce a devastating effect.

STATS

⚔ STRENGTH		4
🛡 DEFENSE		5
👢 SPEED		2
❤ HEALING		1
🔥 MAGIC		1

EQUIPMENT

Diamond Axe	Shield	Fishing Rod	Iron Shovel	Lava Bucket	Flint and Steel	Obsidian	Potion of Fire Resistance	Snowballs
						64		64

ARMOR

	Diamond Chestplate	Diamond Leggings	Diamond Boots

TACTICS

The pyro tank loves fire and can expertly wield a lava bucket so that everyone in the vicinity is scorched. The most defensive character class, the pyro is equipped with obsidian blocks that can be used to create defensive posts or to shore up bases. In hand-to-hand combat, the tank can protect itself with a shield and utilize the axe's deadly cleave attack.

SPECIAL MOVE – HOT AND COLD

The pyro tank quickly digs out a ditch and fills it using a lava bucket, then consumes a potion of fire resistance so they're protected against the deadly pool. When enemies stray too close to the pit, the pyro tank uses snowballs to knock them to their fiery doom.

COMMAND BLOCKS

These clever blocks can be programmed to execute hundreds of commands, resulting in special actions being performed in your game. Among other things they can clone structures, make spawnpoints and keep track of scores.

HOW TO GET A COMMAND BLOCK

You'll be building your minigame in Creative mode, which is the only place that command blocks are available. But they don't appear in your inventory – you'll need to use a command to get one.

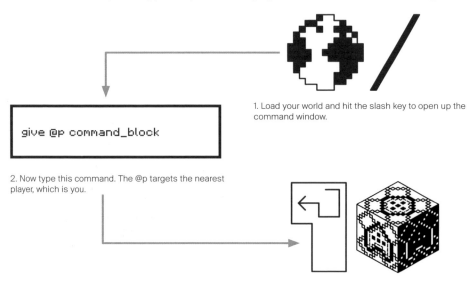

1. Load your world and hit the slash key to open up the command window.

```
give @p command_block
```

2. Now type this command. The @p targets the nearest player, which is you.

3. Hit enter and one command block will appear in your hotbar, ready for use.

IMPULSE COMMAND BLOCKS
This is the default state for all command blocks. Impulse command blocks run their command only once when powered.

CHAIN COMMAND BLOCKS
Chain command blocks only perform a command if the command block that's pointing into it has already performed its command.

REPEAT COMMAND BLOCKS
Repeat command blocks run their command every game tick (0.05 seconds), for as long as they remain activated.

HOW TO USE A COMMAND BLOCK

Place the command block in your world and interact with it. The command block interface will appear, awaiting your instructions.

Type the command you want to execute into the command input window. There's more info about the command options on the following pages.

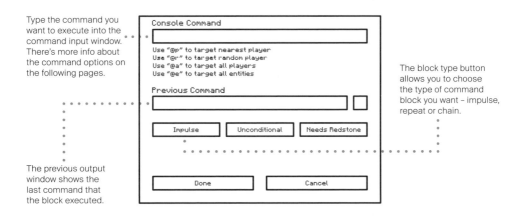

Console Command

Use "@p" to target nearest player
Use "@r" to target random player
Use "@a" to target all players
Use "@e" to target all entities

Previous Command

Impulse   Unconditional   Needs Redstone

Done   Cancel

The block type button allows you to choose the type of command block you want – impulse, repeat or chain.

The previous output window shows the last command that the block executed.

The unconditional button stops the command block from checking that the previous command block in the chain has performed its command. You can change this to conditional, so the command block will perform only if the previous command block performed successfully.

The needs redstone button only runs the command if the block has a redstone power source. You can change this to always active, so the command block will run with or without redstone power. Always active won't work with impulse command blocks – it will just stop them working.

HOW TO POWER A COMMAND BLOCK

The simplest way to provide a command block with a redstone power source is to place a button or a lever on the top or side.

You can also bury the command block in the ground and place a pressure plate on top. It will be activated when a player steps on the pressure plate.

TIP

You must have command blocks set to true on your server properties or they won't work.

USEFUL COMMANDS FOR MINIGAMES

There are several commands that will come in handy when you're creating and playing minigames. Let's take a look at a few of the most useful – you may want to use them for some of the game builds you'll find later in this book.

CLONE

If your minigame involves large amounts of destruction, e.g., Spleef or Gladiator Combat, you'll need to reset the map at the end of each game and restore your creations to their original glory. The clone command allows you to replace the destroyed build with a handy copy that you made earlier. You can use this command without command blocks – let's take a look at how it works.

1 Find the structure that you want to copy. Imagine the structure is sitting inside a large cube, and note the coordinates of two opposite corners of this cube. This is illustrated by the gold blocks.

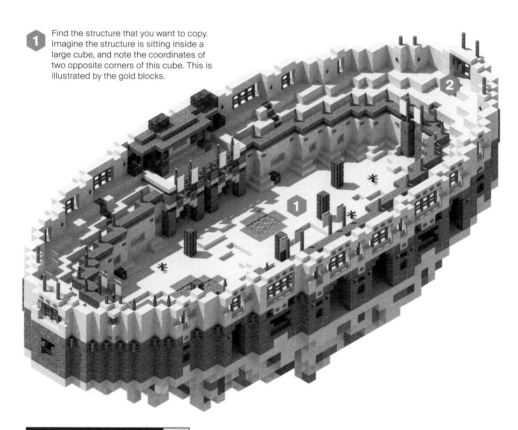

2 Find a good spot to store your backup copy. Check the coordinates for the northwest corner of this area. The sun and moon rise in the east and set in the west, so you can check the sky to work out which direction is northwest.

A copy of your structure will appear in your chosen destination, ready to be copied back to your minigame map when needed. When the time comes, simply repeat the step above but update each set of coordinates so you're cloning the backup copy and putting it back in the right spot on your map.

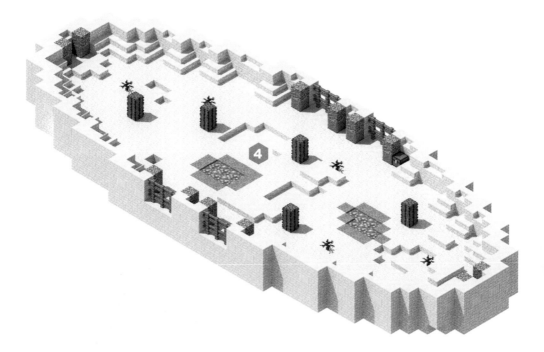

To clone your build, type this command directly into your game. The first two sets of coordinates are the two corners of your existing build, and the third set is the northwest corner of your chosen destination for the copy. "Replace" tells Minecraft to replace any existing blocks in that area with the structure you're cloning.

```
/clone (X Y Z) (X Y Z) (X Y Z)
replace
```

SCOREBOARD

The scoreboard command lets you keep track of team scores and can be incorporated into lots of games for an additional layer of competition. You'll need to set teams, add people to the teams and then add an objective – an action that players have to perform in order to score a point, e.g., mob or player kills. You'll need a suitable spot for your setup – perhaps a lobby outside the arena.

 To set up your first team, open your first command block and type the following command.

```
scoreboard teams add Red
```

 Attach a button to the command block and press it to create the Red team.

 Repeat steps 1 and 2 with your second command block to create your second team. Remember to change the team name.

```
scoreboard teams add Blue
```

 Now you can add players to your teams. Type this command to set up a command block that will add players to the Red team. Add a sign to label the command block so players know what it does.

```
scoreboard teams join Red @p
```

5 Attach a button to this command block. Players who press the button will be added to the Red team. Add a sign to label the command block so players know what it does.

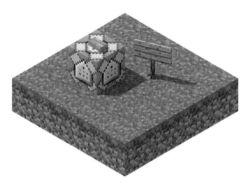

7 Set objectives for team members so that the command block has something to measure. You can record player kills or total kills (players and mobs).

To measure the total number of kills, type the following command into the interface.

```
scoreboard objectives add
kills totalkillCount Kills
```

The middle value (totalkillCount) is what you're measuring, and the final value (Kills) is the name of the objective that will be displayed during the game.

6 Repeat step 3 to set up a command block to add players to the Blue team.

```
scoreboard teams join Blue
@p
```

To measure player kills only, type the following command into the interface.

```
scoreboard objectives add
kills playerkillCount Kills
```

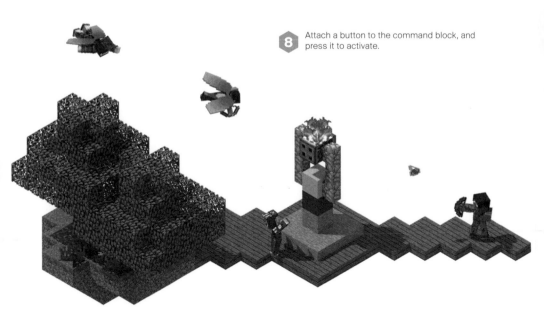

8 Attach a button to the command block, and press it to activate.

9 Decide how each player's kills will be displayed – if you miss this step, player kills won't be registered. There are four display options.

To display player kills as a sidebar during the game, type this into your next command block:

```
scoreboard objectives
setdisplay sidebar kills
```

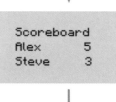

To set the kills to be displayed as a list (a yellow number on the tab menu, where online players are visible), type this command:

```
scoreboard objectives
setdisplay list kills
```

To set the kills to display as a sidebar team color, type this command:

```
scoreboard objectives
setdisplay sidebar.team.red kills
```

Scoreboard	
Red	52
Blue	43

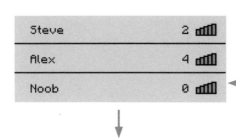

You can also set the display to sit below the player's name (which is visible above their head) using this command:

```
scoreboard objectives
setdisplay belowName kills
```

11 To reset players' scores at the end of a game, type this command:

```
scoreboard players reset @p
```

10 Attach a button to your command block, then press to activate.

When a player presses the button attached to this command block, their score will be reset to 0.

76

SPAWNPOINT

The spawnpoint command is used to set up a spawnpoint for players within a game, so that players find themselves inside your game arena at the press of a button. This comes in handy for games like Spleef, where you don't want to create a traditional entry point.

 Choose a position for your command block (e.g., just outside the arena in a lobby area). Interact with it and type the following command, replacing X, Y and Z with the X, Y and Z coordinates you want to be the starting point for your game. This tells the command block to set the spawnpoint for the nearest player at the coordinates listed.

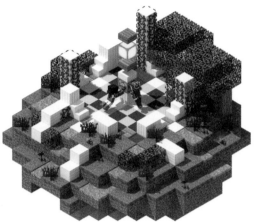

```
spawnpoint @p X Y Z
```

 Add a button to the side of your command block and place a sign next to it that says "BEGIN GAME." When a player presses the button, they will be teleported to the coordinates that you set for the spawnpoint.

CHECKPOINTS

The spawnpoint command can also be used to set up checkpoints in games that have several levels, such as Battle Parkour. This means that if players die they respawn at the last checkpoint they hit, rather than back at the very beginning of the game.

 Decide where you'd like to create checkpoints and place command blocks in each location. The command blocks will need to be buried in the ground so that a pressure plate can be placed on top of them.

 Interact with each command block and type the following command to set a new spawnpoint for the nearest player.

```
spawnpoint @p
```

 Put a pressure plate directly on top of each command block and add a sign next to it that says "CHECKPOINT" so players will know what it is. When a player jumps on the pressure plate, their spawnpoint will be reset to that block. If they die, they will respawn at the last checkpoint they hit.

FINAL WORDS

Hopefully this guide has left you with a brain full of exciting multiplayer ideas to try out with your friends – or enemies! (You can easily transform the former to the latter by relentlessly bragging about your victories – so try to avoid rubbing people's noses in it!) There are as many ways to play Minecraft as there are players – we've just suggested a few. So get out there and mix it up! Invent new Spleef variants, add deadlier conditions to your elytra races, and, wherever you can, find new ways to even things up between players – because the best matches are always the closest! Go get 'em, champ!

MARSH DAVIES
THE MOJANG TEAM

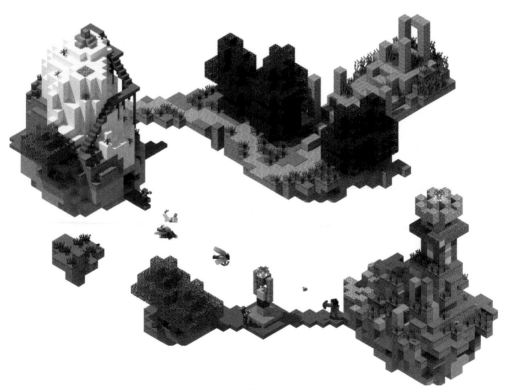

STAY IN THE KNOW!

GUIDE TO:
CREATIVE

GUIDE TO:
EXPLORATION

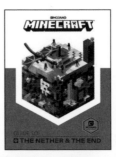
GUIDE TO:
THE NETHER & THE END

GUIDE TO:
REDSTONE

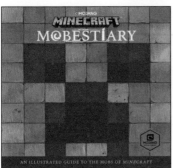
MINECRAFT
M⊙BESTIARY
AN ILLUSTRATED GUIDE TO THE MOBS OF *MINECRAFT*

MINECRAFT
MEDIEVAL FORTRESS
BUILDS

MINECRAFT
THE SURVIVORS'
BOOK OF SECRETS

MINECRAFT
THE ISLAND
NEW YORK TIMES BESTSELLER
MAX BROOKS
AUTHOR OF *WORLD WAR Z*

Learn about the latest Minecraft books
when you sign up for our newsletter at
RANDOMHOUSEBOOKS.COM/MINECRAFT

DEL REY

MOJANG